GUILT

BRENT CURTIS

Dr. Tom Varney
Series Editor

NAVPRESS ●
BRINGING TRUTH TO LIFE
NavPress Publishing Group
P.O. Box 35001, Colorado Springs, Colorado 80935

The Navigators is an international Christian organization. Jesus Christ gave His followers the Great Commission to go and make disciples (Matthew 28:19). The aim of The Navigators is to help fulfill that commission by multiplying laborers for Christ in every nation.

NavPress is the publishing ministry of The Navigators. NavPress publications are tools to help Christians grow. Although publications alone cannot make disciples or change lives, they can help believers learn biblical discipleship, and apply what they learn to their lives and ministries.

Cover illustration: David Watts

All Scripture in this publication is from the *Holy Bible: New International Version* (NIV). Copyright © 1973, 1978, 1984, International Bible Society. Used by permission of Zondervan Bible Publishers.

Printed in the United States of America

FOR A FREE CATALOG OF
NAVPRESS BOOKS & BIBLE STUDIES,
CALL TOLL FREE 1-800-366-7788 (USA)
or 1-416-499-4615 (CANADA)

CONTENTS

FOREWORD

෬

Psychologists, including Christian ones, are in the bad habit of distinguishing between false guilt and true guilt in a way that makes us worry more about relieving the former than the latter. "You're already forgiven. Now forgive yourself," we're regularly exhorted. The implication, of course, is that there's some block to accepting ourselves that has nothing to do with genuine sin. We can't forgive ourselves, we're often told, because guilt feelings with no legitimate basis continue to repeat the message too many of us received in childhood, that we haven't performed well enough to earn acceptance.

I do believe there is such a thing as neurotic guilt. A child raised to think that daily time in the Bible is required to maintain relationship with God may spend his adult life reading the Bible with no joy, only pressure. And that person needs to enter into the reality of grace, which can free him *from* having to read the Bible in order to keep relationship *to* wanting to read the Bible in order to enjoy relationship. The difference is profound.

But our modern focus on false guilt tends to shift attention away from the deep moral guilt within all of us. This moral guilt reflects our intuitive awareness of continued imperfection. And with that shift, we restrict ourselves to the limited joys of feeling released from pressure; and we miss the far richer joy of celebrating forgiveness from sin.

The moment we define our real problem as false guilt from which we need release, we create a view of our struggles as more psychological than spiritual. The insight of a counselor then becomes more vital than the wisdom of the Bible student.

Brent Curtis discusses the problem of guilt within a biblical framework that puts real sin, not imagined badness, at the center of concern. With the wisdom of a biblical counselor, he leads us through a thought-provoking discussion of the struggle with guilt that robs us of joy.

The joy of the Christian, I might add, is something quite different from fun, and even further removed from what we normally think of as happiness. Joy doesn't necessarily feel good. But it always feels hopeful. And it creates a focus on reality beyond oneself.

The obstacles to fun and happiness are more easily dealt with than the hindrance to joy. In this booklet, the author's knife cuts deeply, and it is handled with the precision required to cut out the bad without destroying the potential for good. Freedom from guilt does not come easily, but it creates the freedom to live. Whatever the cost, it's worth it!

INTRODUCTION

&

We've all heard others say, and perhaps have said ourselves, "Boy, do I ever feel guilty about that!" or "She
sure struggles with a guilty conscience." But what do
we really mean when we say we "feel" guilty? What's
going on inside? And how should we respond when we
feel guilty?

This guide is intended to help you answer those
questions. It doesn't offer a simple formula for handling
guilt feelings because God isn't interested in enabling
us to make life work through formulas. Instead, He
invites us into an adventure with Him that is rarely pre-
dictable. This guide offers you a chance to open some
doors that may have long kept you struggling and dis-
tant from God and others.

Use this guide in any one of three ways: (1) on your
own; (2) with a group after prior preparation at home;
or (3) with a group with no prior preparation.

It's amazing how another person's story can spark
insights into our own situation. A discussion group
shouldn't get larger than twelve people, and four
to eight is ideal. If your group is larger than eight,
one way to be sure everyone gets plenty of time to
talk is to divide into subgroups of four to discuss.
This approach can accommodate even a large Sunday
school class.

You'll get the most out of the guide if you use both prior preparation and group discussion. Group members can read the text of a session and reflect on the questions during the week. They might keep a journal handy to jot down thoughts, feelings, and questions to bring to the group time. This approach allows time for participants to recall and reflect on incidents in their lives.

However, a group can also approach the sessions "cold" by reading the text aloud and answering the questions together. If busy schedules make homework impractical, feel free to take this approach.

Finally, if you're using this guide on your own, you'll probably want to record your responses in a journal.

The guide is designed to be covered in six sessions of sixty to ninety minutes each. However, you could spend a lot more time on some questions. If you have plenty of time, you might want to travel through the guide at your group's own speed.

Each session contains the following sections:

A warm-up question. You'll be coming to sessions with your mind full of the events of the day. To help you start thinking about the topic at hand, the sessions begin with a warm-up question. It often refers to what you've observed about the guilt in your life during the previous week. At other times, it invites participants to let the others get to know them better.

Text. You'll find words of insight into the topic in each session. Sometimes the text appears in one chunk; at other times questions fall between blocks of text. You'll probably want someone (or several people) to read this text aloud while the other group members follow along. Alternatively, you could take a few minutes for each participant to read it silently. If you've all read the text before your group meets, you can skip reading it again.

Discussion questions. These will help you understand what you've read and consider how it relates to your own experience and struggles. Each participant's stories will shed light on what the others are going through.

When the text is broken into two or more sections, with questions in between, you should discuss the questions before going to the next section of text.

Many questions ask participants to talk about themselves. Everyone should feel free to answer at his or her own level of comfort. People will often feel some discomfort if a group is really dealing honestly with the issues. However, participants should not feel pressured to talk more personally than they wish. As you get to know each other better, you'll be able to talk more freely.

Prayer. Ideas for closing prayer are offered as suggestions. You may already have a format for praying in your group, or you may prefer not to pray as a group. Feel free to ignore or adapt these ideas.

During the week. In this section, you'll find ideas for trying what you've learned and for observing your daily behavior more closely. Feel free to do something else that seems more helpful.

Process notes. The boxed instructions will help the leader keep the group running smoothly. There are also leader's notes at the back of this guide.

Whether you're a group leader or a participant, or using this guide on your own, you'll find it helpful to read the introduction to this series from the Institute of Biblical Counseling: *Who We Are and How We Relate* by Dr. Larry Crabb. It explains the reasoning behind this series' approach to handling problems.

TWO KINDS OF GUILT

> LEADER: If you have time, give everyone ten to fifteen minutes to verbalize "where they are" as they begin the group.

1. Complete this sentence: I usually find something to feel guilty about . . .

   ❑ At least once an hour.

   ❑ At least once a day.

   ❑ At least once a week.

   ❑ At least once a year.

   ❑ I always feel guilty.

   ❑ I never feel guilty.

   ❑ Other (name it):

WHAT THIS STUDY IS ABOUT

We've all heard others say or have said ourselves, "Boy,
do I have a guilty conscience!" What do we mean when
we say we "feel" guilty? What's going on inside?

Guilt is a primary emotion we seem to struggle
with in our performance before, and relationships
with, God and others. Guilt that we haven't dealt with
spawns a multitude of other emotions and compulsive
behaviors that drain our energy and isolate us from others behind a veil of performance. Struggle with guilt can
often go on for years, if not a lifetime, for religious and
nonreligious people alike.

There are two kinds of guilt: One keeps us hope-
lessly bound in struggles that have nothing to do with
either love for others or the emotional and spiritual freedom that the Bible teaches should be a growing norm
for Christians (Galatians 5:1-6). The other kind of guilt
can be the doorway to true repentance and freedom.

Through this study I'll show how guilt is directly
connected to the experience of shame — of which we will
also identify two different kinds.

In our sessions on guilt, then, we will look at the
sources of what we will call *true guilt* and *false guilt*, how
each of these is related to shame, the functions of the different kinds of guilt, and the solutions that will allow us
to begin living with freedom from guilt.

GUILT: PICTURE NUMBER ONE

When I was about fourteen, one of those incidents
happened that you seem to always remember. My

stepfather was the foreman of a large cattle ranch in northern Idaho, and on one particular morning we were waiting for a neighboring rancher to join us to inspect some of our cattle on horseback. The neighbor was a man I respected and liked. He always took time to kid and talk with me. As he drove up that morning and stepped out of his pickup, my stepfather came out of the horse stables looking furious. One of my jobs was to keep the stables clean, a chore I had intended to complete that afternoon after we returned.

"Brent, I'm not going to tell you again to keep those barns cleaned out. They're a disgrace," he yelled.

I immediately sensed my friend's eyes on me and felt waves of shame and guilt. I ducked into the stables and began cleaning. When my friend stopped in a moment later to tell me it was time to go, I told him without looking up that I wasn't going. I spent the morning cleaning the stables, fighting back anger, loneliness, and tears.

GUILT: PICTURE NUMBER TWO

About two years after my wife and I married, we were going through a tough month or two when we seemed to be constantly at odds. I remember being very angry with her and treating her for days on end with angry silence, which she tried to break through by fixing my favorite meals and other nonverbal efforts. I remember meeting all of her efforts with more silence. I don't remember what the issue was, but I know I wanted to punish her for some relational failure.

After several days of this I walked into the teachers' lounge at the junior high school where we were both employed and saw my wife sitting alone with a look of abject discouragement and sadness on her face. At about the same time, another teacher who knew us both exclaimed about how totally discouraged my wife looked. I felt strong shame and guilt. I left the room before tears could come.

2. These stories illustrate two kinds of guilt. In which of these stories did you feel more sympathetic with me? Why?

3. In which of the two stories did my guilt seem to relate more directly to my *sin against someone else*? Explain.

4. In which of the two stories did my guilt seem to relate more directly to *seeing myself as inadequate* (i.e., to who I am as a person)? How could you tell?

LEADER: Read these two definitions aloud.

DEFINING GUILT

Now let's define the two different kinds of guilt: *true guilt* and *false guilt*. True guilt is the fact—sometimes felt and sometimes not—that *I have wronged another for my own purposes*. While trying to make my life work in my own way without God, I have violated the law of love in Matthew 22:37-40, which Jesus said summarized God's whole law. Thus I am truly guilty before God and before the one I have wronged. I deserve judgment. Love is not just the absence of wrongdoing as defined by legalistic rules. Rather, it is an active sacrificial movement toward others for their good and God's glory. Most of us can recognize how rarely we do that.

False guilt is a felt awareness that *I have not adequately lived up to what I feel are another's expectations,* so I am in danger of being rejected and abandoned by them. I feel false guilt not over my sin against another, but because of my fear of that person's rejection.

TRUE GUILT	FALSE GUILT
I have wronged another for my own purposes.	I have not lived up to what I feel are another's expectations.

5. False guilt is often felt as a "sense of should" over some nonmoral issue. Share a time when you have struggled with guilt. Was it true or false guilt, according to our definitions?

6. a. *(Optional)* Brainstorm a list of situations where people experience guilt (e.g., saying the "wrong" thing at a funeral, realizing that someone at our dinner table needs something that is not on the table, wearing the "wrong" clothes to a party, and so on).

   b. What do we typically do with these guilt feelings?

7. What question(s) do you have about guilt as we begin this study?

LEADER: Write down the group's questions about guilt. These can help you decide what to focus on in your discussions, and you can return to them at the end of your study to see what progress you've made.

STILLNESS

Many groups like to end their meetings with prayer. If your group isn't used to praying aloud together, you may want to try a simple format. Have a few moments of group silence, then each person can pray a sentence or two in a form like this.

- Lord, thanks for _____.

- Father, right now I'm feeling _____, and what I'd really like to know is _____.

DURING THE WEEK

Watch for times when you feel guilty this week. Keep a log of those incidents under two headings: True Guilt and False Guilt.

SHAME:
The Beginning of False Guilt

ॐ

1. What did you learn as you kept track of your guilt feelings during the week? (Did you notice more true guilt or more false guilt? What kinds of things did you tend to feel guilty about?)

We're going to focus on false guilt for the next several sessions. To understand the function and consequences of false guilt, we'll look at its relationship to shame. In this session we'll examine the beginnings of shame, and next time we'll trace the progression from shame to anger to false guilt.

> LEADER: Ask someone to read Genesis 3:1-8 aloud.

¹Now the serpent was more crafty than any of the wild animals the LORD God had made. He said to the woman, "Did God really say, 'You must not eat from any tree in the garden'?"

²The woman said to the serpent, "We may eat fruit from the trees in the garden, ³but God did say, 'You must not eat fruit from the tree that is in

the middle of the garden, and you must not touch it, or you will die.' "

⁴"You will not surely die," the serpent said to the woman. ⁵"For God knows that when you eat of it your eyes will be opened, and you will be like God, knowing good and evil."

⁶When the woman saw that the fruit of the tree was good for food and pleasing to the eye, and also desirable for gaining wisdom, she took some and ate it. She also gave some to her husband, who was with her, and he ate it. ⁷Then the eyes of both of them were opened, and they realized they were naked; so they sewed fig leaves together and made coverings for themselves.

⁸Then the man and his wife heard the sound of the LORD God as he was walking in the garden in the cool of the day, and they hid from the LORD God among the trees of the garden. (Genesis 3:1-8)

2. What were Adam and Eve apparently ashamed of (verse 7)?

3. What did they do as a result of feeling shame?

LEADER: Read this next section aloud. Tell the participants to see if they can grasp the difference between legitimate and illegitimate shame.

TWO KINDS OF SHAME

Just as there is true guilt and false guilt, there is also legitimate shame and illegitimate shame. Legitimate shame is *sorrow over sin*. The shame Adam and Eve felt was not so much a sorrow over their sin as it was a *discomfort with being seen*—not just physically, but emotionally and spiritually. They were aware of being seen as both sinful and needy in each other's eyes—a sort of "knowing that the other knew," which was unbearable. In response they covered their genitals and "hid" their maleness and femaleness from each other and from God (verse 8).

A sentence in their hearts before God went something like this: "We will not acknowledge our real sin and our need for Your mercy. Instead we will make for ourselves disguises to cover who we are and separate ourselves from You."

We'll call this feeling illegitimate shame: *a felt emotional response to being "seen" by a significant person as needy because of my sin or my inadequacy.* This kind of shame comes from the fear of being rejected and abandoned.

TRUE GUILT	FALSE GUILT
I have wronged another for my own purposes.	I have not lived up to what I feel are another's expectations.

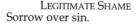

LEGITIMATE SHAME	ILLEGITIMATE SHAME
Sorrow over sin.	Discomfort because someone important sees me as needy.

4. Name some situations that have caused you illegitimate shame. When have you felt, "Now this person knows how bad or inadequate I am! He or she won't want me anymore!"? (For instance, have you felt this when you spilled your drink on someone? When you were caught doing something bad as a child? Did anything in junior high school make you feel like a failure as a man or as a woman?)

19

5. How do we do basically the same thing as putting on fig leaves to cover ourselves?

6. Why do you think Adam and Eve didn't just go to God and explain what they had done instead of hiding?

THREATENED IDENTITY

Instead of openly asking for God's acceptance and mercy in spite of their failure, Adam and Eve hid. Illegitimate shame (which I'll simply call "shame") is the first step in hiding. Even though it doesn't seem so, shame is something I choose that helps me know where to go to get your eyes off my nakedness. It's a way to keep you from seeing me in my need, because seeing my need may cause you to reject me.

TRUE GUILT	FALSE GUILT
I have wronged another for my own purposes.	I have not lived up to what I feel are another's expectations.
↑	↑
LEGITIMATE SHAME	ILLEGITIMATE SHAME
Sorrow over sin.	Discomfort because someone important sees me as needy.
	↑
	I legitimately desire a relationship and fear I can't earn it. You've seen through my identity, with which I've earned our relationship.

20

In my story of the stables in session 1, I was acutely aware of my adult friend seeing my inadequacy. The work ethic was strong in ranching country back in the fifties. I had built an identity as a hard worker because I deeply desired to belong to the world of men. My step-father's remarks threatened to strip my identity from me in front of my friend. I felt foolish, embarrassed, and ashamed.

We feel shame when we're aware of both *a legitimate desire for a relationship* and *the fear that we have insufficient gold to pay for this relationship.*

7. Think again of those incidents of shame you named in question 4. Who witnessed your experience? What identity had you built that you were counting on for relationship? Share your experience with the group.

I was shamed in front of. . . .

My threatened identity was. . . .

STILLNESS

The shame Adam and Eve felt resulted not in a sorrow for their sin but in a felt shame of who they were and a decision to hide from God. But God never asks us to be ashamed of our souls, which are uniquely created in His image. Rather, He asks us to repent of our sinful independence. We'll discover the connection between shame and false guilt in session 3.

As you close in prayer, tell God about how you're feeling. Ask Him to help you understand your shame and guilt this week.

DURING THE WEEK

Pay attention to times when you feel ashamed or guilty. When you notice them, jot a note to yourself about what aspect of your identity is being threatened. (For instance, "I want people at work to think I am highly competent. Mistakes make me look incompetent.")

FROM SHAME TO FALSE GUILT

ॐ

1. What aspects of your identity did you find threatened this week? How did that feel?

Last session we saw that shame arises when we desire a relationship but fear we aren't able to earn it. This time we'll see how that shame leads to false guilt and what false guilt accomplishes for us.

LEADER: Ask someone to read Genesis 3:9-13 aloud for the group.

---

⁹But the LORD God called to the man, "Where are you?"

¹⁰He answered, "I heard you in the garden, and I was afraid because I was naked; so I hid."

¹¹And he said, "Who told you that you were naked? Have you eaten from the tree that I commanded you not to eat from?"

¹²The man said, "The woman you put here with me—she gave me some fruit from the tree, and I ate it."

¹³Then the LORD God said to the woman, "What is this you have done?"

The woman said, "The serpent deceived me, and I ate." (Genesis 3:9-13)

2. What emotions do you think Adam felt toward God and toward Eve (verse 12)?

3. How did Adam and Eve try to handle the true guilt God was confronting them with? Did they seem to feel sorrow for what they had done?

LEADER: As someone reads this section aloud, have participants listen to the progression from shame to guilt.

SHAME TO ANGER

You can almost feel Adam's cloaked anger with God in Genesis 3:12. He felt rage about needing God's mercy. He didn't come right out and confront God with his anger, but instead tried to get God's eyes off him by blaming Him and Eve for what had happened. Often, if not always, the emotion felt after shame is *anger* — anger that I've been put in a position that finds me wanting and endangers a relationship.

As I went to clean the horse stables that morning, I was furious:

■ With myself for wanting relationship

■ With my stepfather for his harshness with me

■ With my friend for seeing my need

If I had unleashed this anger I probably would have screamed at my stepfather and told my friend where he

24

could go. Anger is a dangerous emotion that threatens the loss of all relationship. I think that I must cover it with something that gets me back in control. This is where false guilt functions so efficiently.

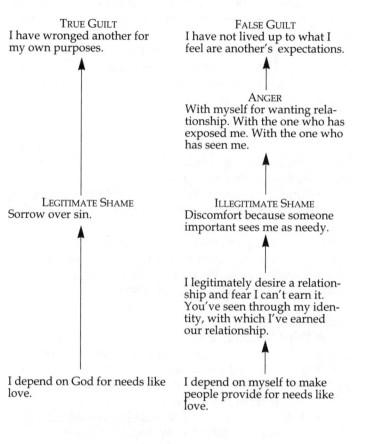

TRUE GUILT
I have wronged another for my own purposes.

FALSE GUILT
I have not lived up to what I feel are another's expectations.

ANGER
With myself for wanting relationship. With the one who has exposed me. With the one who has seen me.

LEGITIMATE SHAME
Sorrow over sin.

ILLEGITIMATE SHAME
Discomfort because someone important sees me as needy.

I legitimately desire a relationship and fear I can't earn it. You've seen through my identity, with which I've earned our relationship.

I depend on God for needs like love.

I depend on myself to make people provide for needs like love.

ANGER TO GUILT

If I had cataloged the progression of my emotions after my stepdad's remark, they would have gone something like this: First, I longed for my friend's acceptance. Nothing is wrong with that. But then, when my friend saw me doing something that might make him stop accepting me, I drowned in shame. That shame was

25

illegitimate; I hadn't sinned. My shame proved I was depending on my friend for my emotional survival. A longing had become a demand.

Next, shame sparked anger with my stepdad—both for the unkindness and harshness of his remark and for threatening to expose my false identity. At the same time I felt anger with my friend for "seeing" my shame.

Lastly, I shifted to guilt over having failed to clean the stables. This entire progression may have lasted a fraction of a second. *By the time I felt guilty I was beginning to get back in control.*

FUNCTIONS OF FALSE GUILT

First, false guilt *covers my anger and inadequacy* so they won't lead to further rejection.

Second, it *tells me what I need to do to stay in control* in the future. For instance, if I just make sure the stables are always clean, I won't be exposed and rejected. I don't have to depend on God or a person I can't control; I can depend on my own performance. Shame tells me I *am* a mistake; something essential is wrong with me. I can't do much about that. But false guilt says I *made* a mistake. I might "survive" if I just avoid repeating that mistake.

A third function of false guilt is to *deny my need to give or receive love.* My guilt covered up my love for my friend and my need for his love in return. It gave him the message that he didn't matter. In this way, I protected myself from pain if he abandoned me.

As I angrily cleaned out the stables, my friend said, "Brent, you know I really like you and have always respected you. Come with us." I felt torn between longing to respond to his words with the knowledge that he really did "see" me and the fear that I would burst into tears if I did respond. I would lose all control if I admitted my need for unconditional love. So I clung to my guilt and mumbled something like, "I don't want to go. I have to get these chores done."

Lastly, false guilt *covers my need for a Savior.* Not

that I was a religious boy at the time or was thinking about this need. But I would have thought I needed a Savior a little less after this incident than I did before. Jesus' invitation to come and have my thirst quenched in Him would have been a little more meaningless than if I had admitted my "thirst" in front of my friend.

4. Think of a time when you felt guilty about something not related to obvious sin.

    a. Are you aware of having felt angry at anyone? At whom?

    b. What did your guilt tell you to do next time in order to avoid rejection?

    c. Whose love for you were you trying to control?

    d. Did you do anything to let the witnesses know their approval didn't matter to you? What?

    e. How did your guilt keep you from having to depend on a Savior to quench your thirst for love?

Soul sentences are things we begin to say to ourselves about what life is like and what we need to do to make life work. They sound like this:

- Life is. . . .

- Life will work if I. . . .

- To survive, I need. . . .

- To survive, I had better not need. . . .

5. What soul sentences might have begun to form inside your heart because of the incident you described in question 4?

6. What sentences like this do you sometimes recognize rumbling around in your heart recently?

DETERMINATION TO BE INDEPENDENT

As I stayed behind that morning, angrily pitching old straw out the stable window, I felt like a victim. I felt the loss of an enjoyable morning doing something I loved and being part of the man's world, but I kept these feelings down with anger. I was angry with myself for failing to complete my chore and for even wanting relationship with these men. The sentence "I don't need them" coalesced and hardened inside.

I felt a determination never to be in a position again where I was found lacking or where my unguarded desire for relationship could be seen. I worked even harder, gaining people's respect from a distance. I developed a style of relating to others that was laid back, underneath which burned a fierce anger and loneliness. If you had asked me if I believed in God at that time in my life, I would have said yes, but my inside sentence would have been more like, "Where is God when you really need Him? I can take care of myself."

7. What was your raw internal reaction to my feelings in the paragraphs above? What sentences do you find yourself empathizing with or reacting to?

STILLNESS

In prayer, tell God about one of your soul sentences — one belief that helps you survive without Him.

DURING THE WEEK

Try to be aware of soul sentences this week. When you find yourself becoming anxious, frustrated, angry, ashamed, or guilty, complete this sentence the way you think your heart is believing:

- Life is _____.

- Life will work if I _____.

- To survive, I need _____.

- To survive, I had better not need _____.

THE SHAME-BASED HOME

૨૨

1. a. Did you come up with any new soul sentences this week? If so, tell some of them to the group.

   b. As you look back at the past week, how would you summarize the primary guiding belief(s) behind your actions? Complete this sentence: Life depends on. . . .

We've seen how depending on self brings shame, and shame leads to anger, and then false guilt. Anyone who wants to live without total dependence on God is going to struggle with shame and guilt. For many of us, however, our natural bent toward shame flourishes a hundredfold in homes where shame is used as a weapon to control us.

LEADER: Read the following section aloud.

VULNERABILITY

We're born into this world with a total dependence
that is both wonderful and terrifying. Unlike animals
that stand, run, and find their own food to supplement
mother's milk within days, we are totally helpless to
provide for our physical needs for years. For our emotional and spiritual well-being, two decades would not
be overstating the case.

The unconditional love and care from our parents
is the lifeblood that invites us to mature. If our environment is reasonably safe, we have a chance of arriving at
adulthood with what feels like a person inside. If not,
we may arrive there feeling hollow, as if we don't exist
without the approval of others.

Even good parents don't love unconditionally. They
have fears and sinful ways of handling being sinned
against, too. The Bible speaks of this in Numbers 27:3,
Deuteronomy 24:16, Psalm 109:14, Jeremiah 3:25, and
Daniel 9:8. But in a shame-based home, parents use
shaming as a terrible weapon to force their children
to kill any part of themselves that is threatening to the
parent.

TEACHING A CHILD SHAME

Several months ago, we had friends in our home who
are also counselors. My eldest son, who was five, was
being particularly demanding that morning. When
Ginny or I asked him to do something, he yelled, "No!"
at the top of his voice. When we reprimanded him, he
threw himself on the floor in a tantrum. I remember
being keenly aware of the eyes of my friends. I felt
acute shame at being a counselor and having such an
unruly son.

I heard the words come out of my mouth, "Drew,
you're a bad boy!" Not "Son, you're behaving badly,"
but "You *are* bad." I knew what I had done immediately, aided by the admonishment of my friend's wife.

Even my son knew something was wrong. "Daddy,

you're not supposed to talk to me that way," he chided. The look on his face expressed confusion and fear. I felt worse than I have in a long time. Later in his room that night, I apologized and invited him to see that sometimes fathers are wrong. It was a good opportunity also to create thirst in him for a Father who does love unconditionally.

We will be using the word *longings* to denote that part of us that legitimately longs for unconditional love and acceptance, for strength that can see us as we truly are and yet not abandon us or need us in wrong ways.

2. What do the following sentences tell the child to do with his or her emotions and longings?

- You're such a selfish child.

- You've never been very strong.

- If you don't stop being such a whiner, I'll give you something to whine about.

- You just don't know how good you have it. Wait until you know what I know.

- You're not really hurt. Now stop that crying.

■ If you ever tell anyone, Daddy and Mommy will have to leave you.

3. a. Were there shame-based sentences in your childhood home? What were they?

    b. What effect did they have on you at the time?

4. *(Optional)* Do you find yourself using sentences like this with your own children or other people? What are you feeling inside just before you use them?

THE TERROR OF ABANDONMENT

The sentences themselves are not so frightening, though they are damaging. It's the threat of abandonment behind them that truly terrifies a child. That threat may lie in a parent's explosive anger, emotional hysteria that asks the child to care for the parent, physical or sexual abuse, emotional unavailability, or actual physical abandonment.

In all of these is a terrifying message that the child will go to any lengths to avoid hearing. The message goes like this: "There is no one in your world who loves you as you hoped, who has the strength to know you and handle you." If the child were sinless, she would say to herself, "This hurts very badly, but I'll put my hope in God to provide the love I need. I really am helpless, but He will protect my soul from destruction." However, the normal child tells himself that he is responsible to get his needs met and protect his world from destruction.

This is where false guilt functions so powerfully.

34

It's like a compass telling me where I cannot go if I want to survive without being abandoned in any or all of the ways I've mentioned. If as a seven-year-old I go to my mother and say, "Mom, I'm bored," and get a furious response of, "You are so selfish. Go find something to do!" I'm going to feel the terror of emotional abandonment. I will not have the insight to see that Mom is afraid too and is handling her fear in sinful ways. I need her too badly. I will begin instead to tell myself that I'm a dull child and not very much fun to be around.

Once I have internalized that belief, *I know what I have to do if I want to control Mom. Boredom is no longer a sign of my thirst for involvement but rather a shameful part of "me" that is "bad."* I begin to "feel guilty" about the fact that I want involvement of a different kind than I am being offered.

I have found a way to survive that controls my world. The part of me that longs for involvement is sentenced to some dark basement room, what Robert Bly in *A Little Book on the Human Shadow* (HarperSanFrancisco, 1988) calls the "bag of shadows." It doesn't die there but begins to ferment and metamorphose.

The reasoning works basically like this:

- There is no one in my world who loves me as I need to be loved.

- It's my job to win love and avoid abandonment.

- If I let people know I'm bored/sad/angry/silly, they'll abandon me.

- I must never be bored/sad/angry/silly.

- My boredom/sadness/anger/silliness is a bad part of me.

5. Where are the flaws in this reasoning?

6. a. Do you recall feeling guilty for longing for attention and affection? What about longing for a parent who was strong and dependable? What situation(s) prompted you to feel guilty?

   b. How did feeling guilty help you avoid being abandoned?

ANGER BEHIND THE GUILT

Most of us can sympathize with the child in the previous illustration. We rightly feel he is the victim of his mother's sinful way of handling her world. What we don't see as clearly are the angry sentences that begin to form in the child's heart and are camouflaged by false guilt. Sentences like, "It's not fair. I hate her. Someone *should* be there for me. The only way to survive in a world like this is to be in control." These sentences also go into "the bag of shadows." The child cannot admit they are there, but inside, he feels like a victim.

What began as a child's way of survival becomes a way of life. He or she develops a style of relating to control others. This relational style is energized by a terrible rage. The rage doesn't necessarily take the form of visible anger; it may simply look like control through certain personality traits. To let his anger be seen could bring about the greatest disaster of all: *abandonment.*

God described the nation of Israel's worship of idols like this:

My people have committed two sins:
    They have forsaken me,
        the spring of living water,
    and have dug their own cisterns,
        broken cisterns that cannot hold water.
    (Jeremiah 2:13)

7. How does this compare to the way we handle our fear of abandonment?

AVOIDING BLAME

Children who grow up in shame-based homes learn early that they must either blame or be blamed. There is no freedom to make mistakes and find the forgiveness that leads to continued relationship. If I am to blame, then the threat of abandonment looms again on the horizon. At all costs I must make sure I am not at fault. False guilt keeps me working hard to make sure that I am not to blame.

8. Are you aware of yourself working hard to make sure you are not to blame? What are some ways in which you do that?

❖ ❖ ❖

LEADER: If your time is limited or if your group contains many single people, you can omit this section on shame-based marriages. Married participants can reflect on this section on their own. This would be a good topic to write about in a journal or for an entire group discussion time. Unmarried people may be able to relate this material to past or present significant friendships.

9. What atmosphere do you think will be present when two people who were raised in shame-based homes come together in a marriage?

SHAME-BASED MARRIAGES

On the surface in shame-based marriages will be consistent if not constant bickering and power struggles over seemingly small issues that happen over and over again without resolution. Anger lurks just beneath the surface, constantly threatening to erupt. Each spouse has developed an elaborate system of manipulation maintained by false guilt to get the other to meet unstated needs. Those needs remain unstated because both spouses feel ashamed of stating them directly. Or they have learned not to even know what they really are.

Each spouse must be perfect in order to get the other to come through for them. The failure of either one to succeed at perfection causes increased rage and hopelessness. Each feels dominated and trapped by the other.

They learned long ago to live by rigid standards and ritualistic behavior that kill legitimate passion. The fear and confusion of a real relationship keep them dead and demanding.

10. What evidence do you see in your marriage of each of the following?

    ■ Lack of spontaneity

    ■ Anger

    ■ Dead-end arguments

11. Spend some time tracing what lies beneath these things. Look for longings and deep feelings you are

uncomfortable expressing. Look for signs of shame, anger, false guilt, the fear of abandonment, and the desire to control. You will probably find yourself asking some hard questions. What does this tell you about yourself? What hope do you see for change in your relationship? What needs can be safely expressed?

❖ ❖ ❖

A HOME WITHOUT SHAME

In a shame-based home, there is no freedom to make mistakes and find the forgiveness that leads to continued relationship. Children in God's household, however, have exactly that kind of freedom.

> If we claim to be without sin, we deceive ourselves and the truth is not in us. If we confess our sins, he is faithful and just and will forgive us our sins and purify us from all unrighteousness. . . . My dear children, I write this to you so that you will not sin. But if anybody does sin, we have one who speaks to the Father in our defense — Jesus Christ, the Righteous One. (1 John 1:8–2:1)

STILLNESS

Talk with God about this freedom to make mistakes. Tell Him how you respond to the promise in 1 John. Do you want to believe it, but it goes against all your experience? Ask Him to help you believe it.

DURING THE WEEK

Be alert for times when you feel guilty this week. Probe beneath that feeling for:

- The fear of abandonment (often felt as rejection at less deep levels).

- Anger at the person who has "made" you feel guilty by threatening abandonment.

- The desire to control yourself and the situation so you won't be abandoned.

- The legitimate longings under all these feelings.

COMPULSIONS, ADDICTIONS, AND ANXIETY:
Stepchildren of Shame and False Guilt

෫෧

1. Did you learn anything this week as you watched for feelings of guilt? For instance, was it usually true guilt or false? Could you identify the anger, fear of abandonment, or desire to control?

A DEEPER LOOK

Longings and feelings camouflaged by shame and false guilt don't just go away. They return stronger than ever in obsessive fantasies or thoughts that are often acted out in compulsive behavior. *Obsessive* means we are unable to stop thinking about something even when we want to. *Compulsive* refers to behavior that doesn't feel like a choice. It seems to be a drive or urge that has a mind of its own. When compulsive behavior begins to dominate and disrupt our daily life in ways that we know are destructive, yet seem unable to stop, we call it *addictive behavior*.

WHERE DOES COMPULSIVE-ADDICTIVE BEHAVIOR ORIGINATE?

When I was fourteen we lived in Idaho, where kids received their driver's license at that early age. Our

41

home at that time was not a safe or open place emotionally. One Sunday, I convinced my parents to let me stay
home from church.

After they had gone I jumped into the old green
Plymouth station wagon that belonged to the ranch
where we lived and drove to town. I ended up at the
local supermarket browsing through the magazine
rack. In the back row was a group of magazines under
the general title of "Police Stories." What they had in
common were cover pictures of scantily clad women
and promises of their "secret lives and stories" inside.
I nervously took one to the check-out stand. To my
amazement the clerk checked me out and sent me on
my way. I was so excited I could hardly breathe.

I remember going to the privacy of my room
and reading through the stories, feeling better than I
had in a long time. It was as if I had been invited into
some intimate place where I could experience feelings
I would be ashamed of in the presence of others. For
several months after that I would find myself at that
magazine rack and others as if drawn there by some
mysterious force.

LEADER: Depending on how safe participants
feel in the group, discuss questions 2 through 4
together or let each person write answers privately.
A third option is to divide into one group of men
and one of women for discussion, since some people feel more comfortable revealing compulsions in
same-sex groups.

2. Are you aware of thoughts or behaviors in your life
   that seem to have a mind of their own? If you can,
   list a few of these on paper. Tell the group about
   any you feel comfortable sharing.

3. *When* do these thoughts and behaviors seem to come on you?

4. *Where* do you tend to struggle with these thoughts and behaviors?

Often the secrecy of these places — where we go to feel good or neutralize pain — gives them much of their power. We have learned to experience emotions there that we would be ashamed of in front of others.

A CYCLE OF GUILT AND SHAME

Events such as the one I described from my own life often begin a cycle of shame, false guilt, performance, and renewed thirst. I thirst for relationship. I try to quench my thirst in some illicit way. Then I feel shame, false guilt, and also true guilt because I really have tried to find life in a wrong way. I try to handle these feelings by some sort of penance (such as promising myself and God never to do it again), and then performance (keeping up with my responsibilities, striving for better behavior, and so on).

The result of all this is a dry legalism that leads to emptiness and renewed thirst, which is then quenched again in an illicit way. Although there are no hard and fast rules as to the direction this illicit thirst-quenching will take, men often seek sexual relief of some sort. Women many times will use food or compulsive house-cleaning to kill the thirst. We might diagram the cycle like this:

Thirst
    Illicit quenching
        Shame
           Guilt
              Penance
                (Performance)
                  Emptiness
                    Dryness
                      (Renewed thirst)

Legalistic religious systems, whether personal or theological, deal with this cycle by *using false guilt to deny or kill the thirst.* This increases the intensity and compulsiveness of the cycle in a never-ending spiral. We can respond in one of two ways: indulgence or anesthesia. *Indulgence,* or giving in to the compulsion, leads eventually to hypocrisy — living a double life — for those with any conscience left or to total reprobation for those who have destroyed their conscience. Many of us prefer to handle the problem by *anesthetizing* our thirst via television, chores, food, Bible study, etc. It appears that we no longer struggle with the compulsion because we've replaced it with a socially approved addiction.

5. Which mode of illicit thirst-quenching (anesthesia or indulgence), do you find yourself most prone to use? If you feel comfortable doing so, tell the group what you do to satisfy or numb your thirst.

PENANCE AND REPENTANCE

Penance is a mockery of repentance. It declares me in control of doing right, avoiding wrong, and paying for my misdeeds. But the only way I can control my compulsions is to hide and kill my thirst, banishing it to that basement room. But that creates even more compulsive-addictive behavior and illicit thirst-slaking.

44

By contrast, true *repentance* requires me to admit my thirst and all the ways I have tried to quench it that don't involve God. By grace, He never asks me to destroy my soul's longings, but to be honest about my thirst and to entrust its quenching ultimately to Him. This *does not* mean that I become an island, denying I need anything from my spouse, children, and friends. That would be another form of protecting myself.

More than one man I've counseled has told me, for instance, that he prayed for the Lord to take away his sex drive, rather than face his wife's anger or emotional distance caused by his sin against her or her own relational problems. (It's usually a combination of both.) This form of false guilt always wears the guise of humility and spirituality, but it refuses to face the fearfulness (including personal shame, guilt, and stubbornness) of what it means to begin loving his spouse differently.

6. a. From whom do you find yourself retreating because of shame and guilt?

   b. What might you have to face if you didn't use guilt as an excuse to retreat?

ANXIETY

Anxiety might be described as "the fear of being found out." It's most often experienced as a free-floating fear and dread not attached to any recognizable source. It is a sense of "something bad about to happen." Anxiety can overwhelm us to the point of paralysis. We may be afraid to get out of bed and in severe cases may drop out of life altogether.

A year ago, my partner in counseling who was a

close friend died in an airline crash. Some weeks after his death, I found myself facing Monday mornings with feelings of dread and anxiety. Once I got into the week they would lessen, and weekends were a time of escape when I tried not to think about anything. But by the next Monday morning the feelings would be back stronger than ever.

As I struggled with these feelings, I came to realize how responsible I felt to be involved with many of the people my friend had counseled and in his ministry endeavors. God's assertion in Psalm 102:23-28 that He truly is the only one who never leaves powerfully encouraged me and opened the door to the real issues I was struggling with.

I realized in an even deeper way how much pressure I have felt all my life to live up to others' expectations so they wouldn't leave. I saw in new ways how the guilt I felt was related to how much I have feared abandonment all my life and how little my efforts had succeeded in getting anyone to stay. (I can't control airline crashes.)

I saw how my efforts at being everything to everybody isolated me from others I cared about, and that the isolation increased my fear and anxiety. I saw with new clarity how much I longed for someone's unconditional love:

- I *deny my longings* for love.

- I feel I must *hide* behind some performance.

- I *isolate* myself so no one will know my failures.

- I'm *anxious* that I'll be found out.

7. Are you aware of fear or anxiety in your life? Describe what happens.

8. a. What are you afraid people will find out?

   b. What might happen if people find that out?

9. a. Can you connect your anxiety to any beliefs about your performance? What are they?

   b. Can you connect them to any longings? What longings?

FACING OUR THIRST

False guilt submerges my true emotions and thirst for relationship. Those feelings then pop up in compulsive behaviors, demanding relief in illegitimate ways. Legalism's response to the cycle of compulsion is some form of penance that kills my thirst. But facing the legitimacy of my thirst and how I have sought to quench it apart from God invites me to look at the true guilt of my independence from Him.

STILLNESS

Talk with God about your thirst for relationship and the ways you try to quench it without Him. Take some time for confessing, either aloud or silently.

DURING THE WEEK

Read and reflect on these scripture passages:

> Psalm 102:23-28
> Isaiah 40:30-31
> Luke 12:4-7
> 1 John 4:13-18

What thoughts and feelings do these passages provoke in you? What might be blocking you from experiencing the hope and safety they describe?

TRUE GUILT:
Gateway to Freedom

28

The goal behind most recovery methods is *wholeness*. While I believe the Lord's goal is that we be whole and entire, lacking nothing (James 1:4), the pursuit of wholeness in itself can cover up the issue of my independence from God. This pursuit often leads to a different end than the wholeness God wants to give us.

By contrast, conviction of our true guilt before God and others leads to brokenness. This kind of brokenness admits that all of our efforts have never gotten us what we're really looking for: the intimacy with God and others Jesus refers to in John 17:20-26. In spite of the pain we have suffered in harmful relationships, the Bible insists that our real problem is the way we have handled being sinned against: our sinful independence from God.

1. Complete this sentence: The thing that most caused me to become a Christian was . . .

   ❑ My life was a mess, and I needed someone to help me.

   ❑ It seemed logical that God created the world and that Jesus is indeed the Savior.

   ❑ I was greatly convicted about the sinfulness of my life.

❑ I was overwhelmed by God's love for me.

❑ I feel like I have always believed.

 Your compelling reason:

Many of us came to Christ not so much out of being totally convinced of our sin as out of an awareness of need. This is legitimate. Jesus invites people to come to Him on the basis of their thirst. However, the Lord exposes more of our real independence as we spend time with Him.

> LEADER: The following story is longer than most of the sections you've been reading aloud. It begins with a story you read in session 1, then continues to recount my journey to true guilt and real change inside me. Let participants read this to themselves, underlining statements that sound like thoughts, feelings, or experiences they've had.

BRIEF CONVICTION

My wife and I were going through a tough time when we seemed to be constantly at odds. For several days I treated her with angry silence, which she tried to break through by nonverbal efforts. I met her efforts with more silence. I wanted to punish her for some relational failure.

During this time I walked into the teachers' lounge at the school where we were both employed and saw my wife sitting alone, looking discouraged and sad. Just then, another teacher commented on how totally discouraged my wife looked. I felt strong shame and guilt, but I left the room before tears could come.

That day I recognized how badly I had been treating her. I felt convicted about my anger toward her and the hurtfulness of my actions. I felt truly sorry and

wanted to love her differently. But when I spoke to
her about my feelings that night, she looked confused
and denied hurting. All my anger was reignited, and
I remember feeling resignation about our relationship.
For the next few days I went back to relating to her at a
certain distance.

My desire to love my wife differently really did
come from conviction of true guilt, I believe. None-
theless, it was not very deep and was swept away by
her closed response. I was very aware of my anger and
sinfulness toward Ginny in the preceding days. But I
was not aware of a style of relating that went back to
my days at my stepfather's ranch.

LOCKED BEHIND THE MASK

I knew nothing of the mask I was living behind when I
married Ginny. I remember coming across as confident
and relaxed, a man who wasn't bothered by much.
Ginny seemed to respond to me, and it felt good to
have that interest from her. I felt that finally I had found
a person who would come through for me and would
allow me to lay aside my mask.

Inside me, the loneliness, insecurity, and anger —
that were there when I was fourteen and younger — were
as intense as ever. So many things were going on inside
that I was afraid to mention or didn't know how to talk
about them. On our honeymoon, I tried to talk about
these things, feeling anger and embarrassment. Ginny,
no doubt shocked by the different man who seemed to
appear out of nowhere, was more interested in talking
about the beauty of the countryside we were passing
through. I interpreted this as evidence that there was a
part of me no one wanted and would never want (not
totally inaccurate) and sank into a semi-depression.

A LONGING DISCOVERED

As the years went by I became aware of a series of relationships where I had felt disappointment — girlfriends,

stepfather, uncles, and friends. I learned that something in me was afraid of intimacy. I was uncomfortable when people tried to be close. However, the death of my biological father brought things to a head.

I remember the day my sister, who had been raised by him, called to tell me of his death. What surprised me was the depth of emotion I felt for a man I really never knew. My mother and stepfather had moved to another part of the country when I was eight, and I saw my father infrequently after that. When I did see him I was less aware of any great longing to be with him than of feeling like an important guest in his home.

In the months after his death I went through a series of emotions for him—from the indifference I had always felt to great anger toward him for abandoning me to feelings of being an orphan longing for a dad. I realized these emotions had been inside me a long time.

I felt like a small, confused boy, afraid and longing for an anchor to trust in. In the following weeks, I cried more than I ever had in my life. I felt deeply alone and paralyzed by the pain welling up that I had always been able to control. The freedom I hoped would come with these feelings eluded me. I vacillated between wanting to write off relationships with everyone I loved and a desperate need to make contact with them at some lost depth.

At the close of every weekend, the feelings of anxiety and dread I mentioned previously would come over me. The prospect of facing another week where anything was required of me seemed overwhelming. I felt more hopeless and lost than ever, like a boy of seven who is required to live in the world of a man of forty.

RAGE ERUPTS

One Saturday afternoon, I was looking through old photos of my father as a young man, which were sent to me by a relative after his death. Some were of a slender man in a U.S. Army uniform. In another, he and my mother appeared cheek to cheek superimposed on a movie screen above the heads of a make-believe audience. For the first time, I felt compassion for my father as a man—a man with his own confusion, hopes, and dreams; a man with his own pain and longings.

My tears for him were interrupted by a rage that came from some long-locked room inside. I found myself cursing God for His seeming lack of care for the generations of our family. Bitter anger and pain flowed out that I knew had originated when I was a young boy. The depth and intensity of the feelings shocked me. It was like meeting a man who had been there all along, but whom I had kept carefully hidden while I tried to appease God through a series of performances. My deepest anger was at Him.

BROKENNESS

I thought perhaps my journey would be over, or at least ready to resume on a higher plane, after the events of that afternoon. I heard no reply from God and saw no vision. If anything, I had a sense of Him as a listening presence.

That difficult year had started with my partner's death. As spring turned to summer, my mother suffered a serious illness requiring a month-long stay in the hospital. Her illness confronted me with her mortality and the distance I often felt from her. Ginny's father came to visit us and suffered a heart attack, requiring open heart surgery. For a while, it seemed he wouldn't pull through.

Going to my counseling office every day, listening to the stories of others, continually reminded me of the loss of my friend, the illnesses of my family, and the fragility of life. Often I felt I should be the one seeking counsel instead of offering it.

One evening in October, three neighborhood friends and I played three matches of doubles tennis as we often did. The next morning I awoke to severe pain in my lower back and leg. Over the next weeks I pursued a variety of chiropractic care, medicines, and cortisone injections in my spine—all to no avail. Sometime in December, I awoke in the middle of the night feeling intense pain. No matter which way I turned I couldn't find a comfortable position.

I had decided that I was going to be honest with God no matter what. I didn't care if He couldn't handle it. Soon enough I found myself spewing out the agony of anger and bitterness about life in general and the events of the last year. When I had completely emptied everything inside, I found myself waiting for an answer. In the stillness that followed I sensed God asking, "Do you want anything?" Just as quickly, my response blurted out, "No! I want nothing from You. The time is long past."

I was again amazed at the intensity behind that statement. For the first time at a passionate level, I knew He wasn't guilty of rejecting me; rather, I was guilty of rejecting Him. That awareness led to one very small prayer, "Father, help me. I really do want You as my Father." For a few moments before I fell asleep that night, I felt a peace and a rest I had not felt perhaps since I was first saved.

2. What did you underline in this story, and why?

3. Did you find anything in this story hard to understand or far outside your experience? Explain.

4. I got angry when Ginny failed to respond warmly to my confession of true guilt. Have you ever done that? Why do you suppose we do that?

5. a. I described feeling grief and loss over not having a father, feeling like a confused little boy looking for someone to trust, feeling deeply alone and paralyzed. Are you aware of feelings inside that would surprise those who know you? Take a minute or two to write some of those down.

   b. *(Optional)* Share some of those feelings with the group, along with what you do with them when you feel them.

   "I know your deeds, that you are neither cold nor hot. I wish you were either one or the other! So, because you are lukewarm — neither hot nor cold — I am about to spit you out of my mouth." (Revelation 3:15-16)

6. In Revelation 3:15-16 Jesus says that what He most wants from us is passion. Do you have any feelings toward Him that could be described as passionate? Are they comfortable feelings? If not, what do you do with them?

7. a. How aware are you of trying to find life independently from God? Are you aware of the kind of hostility toward God that I've described? Explain.

   b. How do you suppose it's possible to genuinely follow Christ for years before discovering this kind of stubborn independence inside?

Jesus had this to say to the religious leaders of His day:

> "Woe to you, teachers of the law and Pharisees, you hypocrites! You are like whitewashed tombs, which look beautiful on the outside but on the inside are full of dead men's bones and everything unclean. In the same way, on the outside you appear to people as righteous but on the inside you are full of hypocrisy and wickedness." (Matthew 23:27-28)

8. It's uncomfortable to face the fact that this might be an accurate description of us. Can you see yourself at all in these words? How?

FACING THE TRUTH

My genuine desire to love my wife differently quickly vanished with her response. As long as I am trying to find life in other people, ultimately I will be a prisoner to their response to me. I will stop loving them as soon as they "abandon" me emotionally or physically.

True deep repentance stems from an awareness that I have rejected God as the source of my life. My true guilt comes from knowing I have always been angry at God and my "love" for others has always been conditioned on their response to me. Brokenness comes from seeing the ugliness of these realities along with facing how little my efforts have gotten me. I believe this was the condition of the prodigal son as he faced his life in the pig sty (Luke 15:11-20).

While false guilt hides the real issues of my heart and the thirst of my soul behind performance, *facing the anger and thirst* in my heart uncovers my true guilt. Where I am really guilty and deserve punishment is in my rebellion against God as the source of my life and the resulting manipulative and unloving way I live with others.

Facing my anger, thirst, and rebellion leads to deep repentance, the acknowledgment that life ultimately comes from God. Such repentance feels like freedom, unlike the constant penance I find myself doing to hide my anger with God and others.

9. *(Optional)* Phariseeism is the ultimate false religion maintained by unrelenting allegiance to false guilt. When we keep ourselves and others preoccupied with rule-keeping, we help both ourselves and others avoid the real issues of our rebellion.

   As you read the passages of Scripture listed below, look for the threads of false guilt and rule-keeping, as opposed to true guilt about running one's own life.

   Luke 11:37-54

   Luke 15:11-32

   Luke 18:9-14

   [10]For there are many rebellious people, mere talkers and deceivers, especially those of the circumcision group. [11]They must be silenced, because they are ruining whole households by teaching things they ought not to teach—and that for the sake of dishonest gain. [12]Even one of their own prophets has said, "Cretans are always liars, evil brutes, lazy gluttons." [13]This testimony is true. Therefore, rebuke them sharply, so that they will be sound in the faith [14]and will pay no attention to Jewish myths or to the commands of those who reject the truth. [15]To the pure, all things are pure, but to those who are corrupted and do not

57

believe, nothing is pure. In fact, both their minds and consciences are corrupted. [16]They claim to know God, but by their actions they deny him. They are detestable, disobedient and unfit for doing anything good. (Titus 1:10-16)

In Titus 1:10-16, Paul warned Titus about some trouble-some teachers. They were teaching that people had to believe certain Jewish myths and obey manmade laws in order to have a real relationship with God (verse 14). They said moral purity depended on keeping the rules. Paul countered that a person wrapped up in rule-keeping to earn God's acceptance would never feel pure—would never even be pure—while those who had confessed and repented their ways of trying to earn life possessed a deep and genuine purity. Acts 10:9-15 portrays the same truth.

10. *(Optional)* How do you think Paul's message, especially Titus 1:15, applies to our discussion of false guilt?

STILLNESS

In Matthew 6:7-8, Jesus encourages us to talk simply to Him, not worrying about making our prayers sound impressive to ourselves or others. A good way to close this session would be for each participant to have a chance to say a few things to God about what they've learned, how they are feeling about it, and what they would like God to do in them.

CONCLUSION

৯৯

Many of the books, workshops, and support groups
from the codependent movement do a good job in
helping people get in touch with repressed and denied
emotions as well as ways in which individual people
develop unhealthy dependencies on others. What they
sometimes fail to address is the rebellion underneath
these dependencies. To understand this rebellion we
must bring God into the picture as the One being
rejected.

One clear picture of what false guilt is all about is
found in the book of Job. Hearing of Job's calamities, his
friends come to comfort him. When they see his condition, they are grieved and tear their clothes. For seven
days they sit with him in mourning and say nothing
(Job 2:11-13).

Inside, though, they obviously are increasingly
troubled with Job's assertions of innocence. If he really
has not sinned in some way to bring all this calamity on
himself, then whose fault is it?

God answers that question in no uncertain terms
by making it clear that *He* is God (Job 38–41). He does
not blame Satan, apologize, or really even empathize
at that point. Yet confronted with God Himself, Job
goes away enlightened and apparently comforted. God
rebukes the friends (Job 42:7-8). Why?

They would rather have imposed guilt on Job than deal with a God they could not understand or control. This is the core issue behind all false guilt: "I will make others responsible or *I* will be responsible, but I will not face any relationship where there seem to be no ground rules under my control."

At one level God rebuked Job's friends for claiming to speak for Him. At a deeper level He was addressing their independence and lack of relationship with Him. This was their true guilt. I believe He asked Job to pray for them to emphasize their independence from Him. They had to see their problem before they could be reconciled.

Independence from God and all the manifestations of that condition is my real problem, my true guilt, according to the Bible. It is this that Christ died to save me from. I expect to find judgment and, instead, find the father portrayed in the parable of the prodigal son. He is running to meet me with tears of joy, a ring for my finger, a robe, and a kiss—a party to celebrate life where death was expected (Luke 15:11-32).

HELP FOR LEADERS

ᔧ

This guide is designed to be discussed in a group of from four to twelve people. Because God has designed Christians to function as a body, we learn and grow more when we interact with others than we would on our own. If you are on your own, see if you can recruit a few other people to join you in working through this guide. You can use the guide on your own, but you'll probably long for someone to talk with about it. On the other hand, if you have a group larger than twelve we suggest that you divide into smaller groups of six or so for discussion. With more than twelve people, you begin to move into a large group dynamic, and not everyone has the opportunity to participate.

The following pages are designed to help a discussion leader guide the group in an edifying time centered on God's truth and grace. You may want one appointed person to lead all the sessions, or you may want to rotate leadership.

PREPARATION

Your aim as a leader is to create an environment that encourages people to feel safe enough to be honest with themselves, the group, and God. Group members should sense that no question is too dumb to ask, that the other participants will care about them no matter what they reveal about themselves, and that each person's opinion is as valid as everyone else's. At the same time, they should know that the Bible is your final authority for what is true.

As the group leader, your most important preparation for each session is prayer. You will want to make your prayers personal, of course, but here are some suggestions:

- Pray that group members will be able to attend the discussion consistently. Ask God to enable them to feel safe enough to share vulnerable thoughts and feelings honestly, and to contribute their unique gifts and insights.

- Pray for group members' private times with God. Ask Him to be active in nurturing each person.

- Ask the Holy Spirit for guidance in exercising patience, acceptance, sensitivity, and wisdom. Pray for an atmosphere of genuine love in the group, with each member being honestly open to learning and change.

- Pray that your discussion will lead each of you to obey the Lord more closely and demonstrate His presence to others.

- Pray for insight and wisdom as you lead the group.

After prayer, your most important preparation is to be thoroughly familiar with the material you will discuss. Before each meeting, be sure to read the text and answer all of the questions for yourself. This will prepare you to think ahead of questions group members might raise.

Choose a time and place to meet that is consistent, comfortable, and relatively free from distractions.

Refreshments can help people mingle, but don't let this consume your study and discussion time.

LEADING THE GROUP

It should be possible to cover each session in sixty minutes, but you will probably find yourself wishing you had two hours to talk about each group member's situation. As you conduct each session keep the following in mind.

Work toward a safe, relaxed, and open atmosphere. This may not come quickly, so as the leader you must model acceptance, humility, openness to truth and change, and love. Develop a genuine interest in each person's remarks, and expect to learn from them. Show that you care by listening carefully. Be affirming and sincere. Sometimes a hug is the best response—sometimes a warm silence is.

Pay attention to how you ask questions. By your tone of voice, convey your interest in and enthusiasm for the question and your warmth toward the group. The group members will adopt your attitude. Read the questions as though you were asking them of good friends.

If the discussion falters, keep these suggestions in mind:

- Be comfortable with silence. Let the group wrestle to think of answers. Some of the questions require thought or reflection on one's life. Don't be quick to jump in and rescue the group with your answers.

- On the other hand, you should answer questions yourself occasionally. In particular, you should be the first to answer questions about personal experiences. In this way you will model the depth of vulnerability you hope others will show. Count on this: If you are open, others will be too, and vice versa. Don't answer every question, but don't be a silent observer.

63

- Reword a question if you perceive that the group has trouble understanding it as written.

- If a question evokes little response, feel free to leave it and move on.

- When discussion is winding down on a question, go on to the next one. It's not necessary to push people to see every angle.

Ask only one question at a time. Often, participants' responses will suggest a follow-up question to you. Be discerning as to when you are following a fruitful train of thought and when you are going on a tangent.

Be aware of time. It's important to honor the commitment to end at a set time.

Encourage constructive controversy. The group members can learn a great deal from struggling with the many sides of an issue. If you aren't threatened when someone disagrees, the whole group will be more open and vulnerable. Intervene when necessary, making sure that people debate ideas and interpretations, not attack each other's feelings or character. If the group gets stuck in an irreconcilable argument, say something like, "We can agree to disagree here," and move on.

Be someone who facilitates, rather than an expert. People feel more prone to contributing with a peer leader than with a "parent" leader. Allow the group members to express their feelings and experiences candidly.

Encourage autonomy with the group members. With a beginning group, you may have to ask all the questions and do all the planning. But within a few meetings you should start delegating various leadership tasks. Help members learn to exercise their gifts. Let them start making decisions and solving problems together. Encourage them to maturity and unity in Christ.

Validate both feelings and objective facts. Underneath the umbrella of Scripture, there is room for both. Often, people's feelings are a road map to a

64

biblical truth. Give them permission for feelings and facts.

Summarize the discussion. Summarizing what has been said will help the group members see where the discussion is going and keep them more focused.

Don't feel compelled to "finish." It would be easy to spend an entire session on one or two questions. As leader, you will be responsible to decide when to cut off one discussion and move to another question, and when to let a discussion go on even though you won't have time for some questions. If there are more questions than you need, you can select those that seem most helpful.

Let the group plan applications. The "During the Week" sections are suggestions. Your group should adapt them to be relevant and life-changing for the members. If people see a genuine need that an application addresses, they are more likely to follow up. Help them see the connection between need and application.

End with refreshments. This gives people an excuse to stay for a few extra minutes and discuss the subject informally. Often the most important conversations occur after the formal session.

DURING THE FIRST MEETING

You or someone else in the group can open the session with a short prayer dedicating your time to God.

It is significant how much more productive and honest a discussion is if the participants know each other. The questions in this session are designed to help participants get acquainted. You can set an example of appropriate disclosure by being the first to answer some questions. Participants will be looking to you to let them know how much honesty is safe in this group. If you reveal your worst secrets in the first session, you may scare some people away. Conversely, if you conceal anything that might make you look bad, participants will get the message that honesty isn't safe.

At some point during the session, go over the following guidelines. They will help make your discussion more fruitful, especially when you're dealing with issues that truly matter to people.

Confidentiality. No one should repeat what someone shares in the group unless that person gives permission. Even then, discretion is imperative. Be trustworthy. Participants should talk about their own feelings and experiences, not those of others.

Attendance. Each session builds on previous ones, and you need continuity with each other. Ask group members to commit to attending all six sessions unless an emergency arises.

Participation. This is a *group* discussion, not a lecture. It is important that each person participates in the group.

Honesty. Appropriate openness is a key to a good group. Be who you really are, not who you think you should be. On the other hand, don't reveal inappropriate details of your life simply for the shock value. The goal is relationship.

Following are some perspectives on a few questions from the sessions, in case your group finds any of them difficult to answer. These are not necessarily the "right" answers, but they should provide food for thought.

SESSION ONE

If group members don't already know each other, you may want to set aside some time for them to get acquainted. You'll be talking about your personal lives in this study, and participants will understandably want to know who they are talking to.

If you have a lot of time, an ideal way to break the ice would be to give everyone ten to fifteen minutes to share "where they are" as they begin the group. They can say anything they want about the last three days or the last three years. The only restriction is that you will call time at the end of ten (or fifteen) minutes. It may take one or two meetings before you even begin with the material in this guide, but you'll find it to be time well spent.

If you have less time, invite group members to begin opening up at a safe level. Question 1 is a low-threat introduction. You should answer first to set the tone.

Questions 2-4. Picture 1 portrays false guilt—I felt guilty about failing to meet my stepfather's standards, not about sin. Picture 2 displays true guilt—I saw I had been sinning against my wife.

Questions 5-6. The goal here is to make sure participants clearly understand the difference between true and false guilt.

Question 7. This guide will address these questions, among others: How can I tell when I should feel guilty and when I shouldn't? Why do I feel false guilt? How can I stop feeling false guilt? What should I do when I feel false guilt? What should I do when I feel true guilt?

Stillness. We've included ideas for prayer in every session. They are just suggestions; feel free to modify them. Praying aloud together may not be appropriate in some beginning groups, such as those that include nonChristians.

During the Week. Likewise, the suggestions for "homework" are also just possibilities. Other good ideas may surface during the course of your discussion. Do encourage everyone to do something with the material during the week because lasting change will be unlikely if the concepts are forgotten from one meeting to the next.

SESSION TWO

Questions 2-3. The text says they were ashamed of their physical nakedness, so they made body coverings. So the question is, why did physical nakedness suddenly become shameful? It seems as though behind the shame of physical nakedness is a shame for one's gender and one's inner self. Adam and Eve refused to be ashamed about genuine sin, so they transferred their shame to their bodies, their sexuality, their personhood.

Question 4. Adolescence raises a great many issues of illegitimate shame. A child is suddenly aware that everyone is evaluating him or her against standards of a perfect male or female body, a perfect mind, perfect study habits and achievements, perfect "coolness" or conformity to culture, perfect talent in sports, music, and so on. There are so many standards that it's impossible for anyone to be adequate according to all of them.

Question 5. Clothes, cosmetics, and hairstyles can all be used to project an image to cover up our feelings of inadequacy. So can cars, homes, and other possessions, academic degrees, professional accomplishments, and a host of other things. These can be valuable things and deeds, but we misuse them as fig leaves to hide our shame.

Question 6. Confession requires humility, a heart that wants to be intimate with God more than it wants to be right, perfect, strong, clever, or adequate. Adam and Eve were proud; they didn't want God's "charity."

SESSION THREE

Question 3. The chief thing a sinful heart wants to avoid is confronting real sin. One of the great things about shame and false guilt (from a sinful point of view) is that they can distract everyone except God from true guilt. Accusations and shifting blame are effective smoke screens. Anger is the emotion behind them.

Question 6. These are possibilities: "Life is unfair." "Life will work if I work hard enough." "To survive, I need to stay in control of my emotions." "To survive, I had better not need anybody's love, or at least not let anybody know I need it."

SESSION FOUR

Questions 2-3. Shame-based sentences tell a child to kill, suppress, or at least hide his longings. His longing for time with Mom is "selfish," not normal. His longing for approval meets the judgment that he's weak. His frank expression of longings is whining. His longing for love is ungrateful and ignorant. His longing for comfort when hurt is minimized. His longing to be secure meets a threat that he must keep secrets or be assured of abandonment.

Sentences like these cause a child to live in constant fear of losing all love, to do anything he can to avoid abandonment, and to numb his longings any way he can.

Question 7. Instead of trusting God to be the One we can always trust not to abandon us, we look for ways to cause people to love us. Pursuing those ways is like digging broken cisterns — trying to meet our needs without God. We turn people or things into idols that we hope will provide us with life.

SESSION FIVE

This session touches on some issues many people won't want to talk about openly. You'll want to assess your group members' comfort and trust levels before you decide how to handle it. People often benefit greatly from being able to confide in someone about obsessive thoughts and compulsive actions, but your entire group may not be an appropriate forum for this. You might encourage participants to meet with one other group member during the week to discuss issues that seemed inappropriate for the whole group.

SESSION SIX

It's not easy to understand how a person can be both a devoted follower of Christ and a raging rebel. Even when our wills have surrendered to Christ, large sections of our hearts fight on in fury. Few of us have grown beyond this double-mindedness. We are all hypocrites to some degree. However, we take a crucial step beyond the Pharisees when we acknowledge our hypocrisy before God and other believers.

The chief goal of this session and the entire study, then, is to encourage participants to start facing their anger, thirst, and rebellion.